THE BECOMING

A Guided Journey Back to the Girl You Once Were

The Becoming

A Guided Journey Back to the Girl You Once Were

K. Nicol

Storyhouse™ Publishing
knstoryhouse.com

THE BECOMING

A Guided Journey Back to the Girl You Once Were

Published by Storyhouse™ Publishing
Houston, Texas
knstoryhouse.com

ISBN (Paperback): 979-8-9940945-0-1
ISBN (eBook): 979-8-9940945-1-8

Cover & Interior Design: Storyhouse™ Design Studio
Chrysanthemum Emblem © Storyhouse™
Wax Seal © Storyhouse™

Printed in the United States of America

First Edition, 2025

DISCLAIMER

This workbook is intended for personal reflection, journaling, and emotional exploration.

It is **not** a substitute for professional mental health care, counseling, therapy, or medical treatment.

If you are experiencing emotional distress, trauma, or any mental health challenges, please seek support from a licensed mental health professional, counselor, or medical provider.

Nothing in this workbook should be interpreted as legal, psychological, clinical, or medical advice. Using this workbook does not create a therapist–client, counselor–client, or attorney–client relationship with the author or the publisher.

Move gently. Take breaks when needed.
Your healing deserves proper support wherever it is needed.

Storyhouse™ Publishing | Raised by 1912

Dedication

For Mama (grandma), born in 1912,

who taught me that strength can be gentle

and gentleness can be strong.

For my children, who continue the story.

And for every woman returning home to herself—

may you find tenderness waiting for you there.

Opening Affirmation

"I move at the pace of my own becoming.
I honor the girl I once was,
and I welcome the woman I am becoming."

A Letter to You

There is a moment in every woman's life when she feels the quiet tug of her younger self—the girl she used to be, the girl she may have forgotten, the girl who still remembers everything.

This workbook was born from that tug.

The Becoming is not meant to rush you, fix you, or require you to be anything other than who you already are. It is a gentle invitation back to your own truth—to sit with your story, to honor the parts of you that survived, and to give voice to the parts that were never allowed to speak.

As you move through these pages, may you take your time. May you breathe deeply. May you allow softness to return to places that learned to harden too soon. And may you trust that every reflection, every memory, every letter, and every quiet revelation is part of your becoming.

Thank you for letting this book hold you.

With love,
K. Nicol
Storyhouse™

HOW TO USE THIS WORKBOOK

A Gentle Beginning

This workbook was created to be a quiet companion — one that walks beside you, not ahead of you, and never behind.
There is no right or wrong way to move through these pages.
There is only your way.

Move Slowly

Healing rarely asks for speed.
It asks for presence.
Read each prompt with softness and allow whatever rises — memories, sensations, emotions, silence — to meet you where you are.
Some pages may feel light. Others may feel heavy.
Both belong here.

Listen for the Girl You Once Were

Throughout The Becoming, you'll meet her — the younger version of yourself who still holds pieces of your story.
Let her speak without interruption.
Let her remember in her own voice.
Let her feel safe on the page.

Let This Be a Sacred Space

Write in the margins.
Circle words that move you.
Pause when something stirs.
Return only when you're ready.
These pages hold no urgency.
They are here to hold you.

Move in Seasons

You may complete this journey in one stretch, or visit it in seasons. Let your emotional capacity — not your schedule — guide your pace. If you feel resistance, that is simply your heart signaling the need for gentleness.

Be Honest, Even When It's Tender

Honesty opens the pathway to healing.
You are not required to be poetic, perfectly expressive, or "strong." You are only asked to be truthful with yourself.

Deepening Your Becoming

Healing is not a destination. It is a continued homecoming. Revisit prompts that feel important. Rewrite earlier pages with new insight. Allow the work to grow as you grow.

Create Ritual as You Move

Light a candle. Play soft music. Sit near a window.
Or simply breathe before you begin.
Ritual creates safety — a signal to your inner world that this is a protected place.

If Something Feels Too Heavy

Pause. Step away. Place your hand over your heart.
Say to yourself:
"I can return when I feel ready."
There is no deadline.
Your healing is not late.

A Final Note

This workbook is an invitation — a slow walk back home to yourself. Move through it with tenderness and curiosity.

Your becoming is already in motion.

Table of Contents

=== PAGE BREAK ===

PART I — RETURNING TO YOURSELF

=== PAGE BREAK ===

PART II — THE LETTERS

=== PAGE BREAK ===

PART III — THE BECOMING

Closing Pages

Chrysanthemum watermark appears softly on section openers.

PART I — RETURNING TO YOURSELF

THE QUIETING

Before you write a single word, take a moment to settle into your body.

A Simple Grounding Practice

1. Sit comfortably.
2. Place both feet on the floor.
3. Take three slow breaths.
4. Whisper your name out loud.
5. Whisper your younger self's name next.

Let the line between you and her soften.
Let her know: "*I'm here. I'm listening. We are safe now.*"

HOW TO USE THE PROMPTS

When a prompt feels heavy, write slowly.

When a prompt feels light, explore freely.

If you feel blocked:

- Write one sentence.
- Write one word.
- Doodle.
- Come back tomorrow.

There is no wrong answer.

There is only your truth — in whatever form it arrives.

CREATING YOUR SOFT SPACE

A Quiet Corner
Not perfect. Not aesthetic.
Just a corner where you can hear your own voice.

A Pen You Love
Ink carries energy. Choose a pen that feels smooth, steady, or safe.

A Soft Time of Day
Early morning stillness.
Late-night quiet.
Or any moment when your nervous system feels open.

Your Honesty
This journey is not about perfection. It's about truth — the kind that frees you.

Your Permission
To pause.
To cry.
To remember.
To feel joy.
To walk away and return whenever you need to.

Optional Companions

- A candle
- A warm drink
- A blanket
- Soft background instrumental music

WHAT YOU MAY FEEL ALONG THE WAY
EMOTIONAL GUIDE

Healing does not follow a straight line. Expect your heart to move in curves, spirals, pauses, and breakthroughs.

You may feel…

Tenderness
Old stories rising with new clarity.

Resistance
A younger part of you whispering, "Is it safe?"
(Yes. You get to move at your pace.)

Relief
Finally naming things you long carried alone.

Joy
As you reconnect with versions of yourself who never stopped waiting for you.

Grief
For the moments you needed more — from life, from others, from yourself.

All of these feelings belong.
Let them come.
Let them teach.
Let them pass through you gently.

Meeting the Girl You Once Were

Close your eyes and imagine you are walking down a familiar path –
one that feels warm, safe, and touched by soft sunlight.

You see a small figure ahead.
She is sitting quietly, waiting.
As you walk closer, you realize it's her –
the little girl you used to be.

Notice her expression.
Her posture.
Her small hands.
The way she looks up at you, curious and hopeful.

She recognizes you instantly.
Not as a stranger – but as someone she has needed for a very long time.

Sit beside her.
Let her speak without interruption.
Let her silence speak too.
She may not use words, but she always tells the truth.

Look at her face.
Notice the softness in her eyes, the innocence in her smile,
the dreams she has tucked away, the fears she carries quietly.

Ask her gently:
"What do you need me to know?"
And wait for the first thing that comes to your heart.

Trust it.
She always answers honestly.

When you feel ready, open your eyes and begin the reflections below.

Who she was:

How she felt most days:

What she wished someone would notice:

What I now understand about her:

What she needed then that I can give her now:

A LETTER TO THE GIRL YOU ONCE WERE

My sweet girl,

I have not forgotten you.

There were moments when you carried more than any child should, and yet you still found ways to laugh, to hope, to glow.

I'm coming back for you — page by page, memory by memory. I'm here now, with the gentleness you deserved then.

You can rest your story in my hands.
I will hold it with honor.

PART II
THE LETTERS

LETTER 1 — When She Felt Different

Before you write to her, take a breath.
Think of the girl who felt "different" long before she understood why.
Different from her friends.
Different from her siblings.
Different from the world around her.

She didn't have words for it then —
only a quiet knowing that she didn't quite fit the shape others tried to place her in.

This letter is for the girl who carried that feeling alone.

A Gentle Introduction

There were moments in childhood when she looked at other kids and wondered,
"Why don't I feel the way they feel?"
Maybe she was quieter. Or too observant.
Maybe she felt too deeply and didn't know what to do with all that emotion.

Maybe she watched everything...
and everyone...
and tried to understand where she belonged.

This chapter is your chance to sit beside her and tell her the truth:

She was never meant to fit in.
She was meant to stand out in her own quiet, beautiful way.

Write to the version of you who felt different.

Tell her what you now understand:
that her uniqueness was not a flaw,
that her sensitivity was a gift,
and that she belonged to herself long before she ever
belonged to the world..

You may begin with:
"My love, you weren't wrong for being different..."

Use these if you'd like a little guidance before writing your letter:

What made her feel different?

What do you now appreciate about that difference?

What would you tell her to help her feel less alone?

How did her "differentness" shape the woman you became?

Letter to the Little Girl Who Felt Different

LETTER 2 — When She Tried to Be Strong

Before you write, take a moment to remember her —
the little girl who tried to be strong long before she should have.

She held things together that were too heavy.
She smiled when she wanted to cry.
She learned to stay quiet, to be helpful, to take care of things…
even when she was the one who needed care.

This letter is for her —
the girl who thought strength meant silence.

A Gentle Introduction

There were times she felt like she had no choice but to be strong.
Maybe she didn't want to burden anyone.
Maybe she thought no one would understand.
Maybe being strong was the only way she felt she could survive the moment.

What she didn't know was this:

Her strength was never measured by how much she carried.
It was measured by how much her little heart endured.

She deserved softness.
She deserved comfort.
She deserved someone to tell her she didn't have to hold it all together.

That someone is you — now.

Write to the version of you who grew up too fast.

Tell her she didn't fail when she struggled.
Tell her she didn't have to be the strong one.
Tell her she deserved arms around her,
not weight on her shoulders.

You may begin with:
"My love, you were never meant to carry so much..."

Use these if you'd like a little guidance before writing your letter:

What moments made her feel like she had to be strong?

What did she hold inside to protect others?

What would you give her now that she didn't receive then?

How did her strength shape the woman you became?

Letter to the Little Girl Who Tried to Be Strong

LETTER 3 — When She Needed Protection

Before you begin, take a slow breath. Think of the little girl inside you — the one who needed someone to stand between her and the world. The one who needed protecting long before she even knew what that word meant.

Maybe she needed protection from chaos.
Maybe from expectations.
Maybe from loneliness.
Maybe from hurt that came too early, too silently, too deeply.

This letter is for the girl who deserved someone to shield her… and didn't always have that.

A Gentle Introduction

There were moments she felt unsafe — emotionally, spiritually, sometimes physically.
Moments where she needed someone to say:

"You don't have to face this alone."
"You're safe with me."
"You deserve to be protected."

But she learned too young that she had to hold herself together. She learned to hide fear behind strength, to pretend she wasn't overwhelmed, to stay small, quiet, or brave in ways no child should have to.

And yet — she survived.

Now it's your turn to stand guard for her. To give her the safety she never had. To be the protector she needed.

Write to the little girl who felt unprotected.

Tell her you see her.
Tell her you believe her.
Tell her she deserved safety, softness, and someone who would have chosen her, every time.

You may begin with:
"My love, you should have been protected..."

Use these if you'd like a little guidance before writing your letter:

What made her feel unsafe or unprotected?

What did she fear most in those moments?

Who should have protected her but didn't?

What protection can you give her now that she never received then?

Letter to the Little Girl Who Needed Protection

LETTER 4 — When She Wanted to Be Loved

Before you write, touch the memory of her gently — the little girl who just wanted to be loved.
Not conditionally.
Not when she was useful.
Not when she was quiet or "good."

Just loved. As she was.

She wanted love that didn't make her shrink, perform, or prove anything.

This letter is for the girl who longed for the love she deserved.

A Gentle Introduction

There were moments she wondered:

"Am I lovable?"
"Am I enough?"
"Do I matter to anyone?"

Little girls shouldn't have to wonder those things. But she did.

Maybe the love around her was inconsistent.
Maybe she felt ignored.
Maybe she felt invisible.
Maybe the people she needed most didn't know how to offer emotional warmth.
Maybe they loved her, but not in the way she needed.

So she began to adapt — to earn love, to chase it, to overgive, to overperform.

What she never knew is this:

She was worthy of love simply because she existed.
And she still is. Now it's your turn to tell her that.

Write to the little girl who wanted to be loved.

Tell her she is lovable, she is worthy,
and she didn't have to earn anything.
Tell her that love should have felt warm, not heavy…
safe, not confusing…
consistent, not conditional.

You may begin with:
"My love, you were always worthy of being loved…"

Use these if you'd like a little guidance before writing your letter:

When did she first question her worthiness of love?

How did she try to earn love or prove herself?

What type of love did she need that she didn't receive?

What do you now know about love that she didn't?

Letter to the Little Girl Who Wanted to Be Loved

Letter 5 — When She Lost Herself

Before you begin, close your eyes and think of her — the little girl who slowly, quietly, unintentionally lost pieces of herself trying to fit into places that weren't made for her.

She didn't wake up one day and decide to disappear.
It happened softly…
through expectations, survival, silence, and moments when she felt she had no choice but to become what others needed.

This letter is for the girl who lost herself before she ever had the chance to fully become herself.

A Gentle Introduction

There was a time she was bright, curious, expressive, and full of wonder.
But life has a way of dimming little girls who shine too brightly.

Maybe she learned to hide her voice.
Maybe she muted her opinions.
Maybe she shrank her personality.
Maybe she silenced her needs.
Maybe she became who others wanted, praised, or depended on.

Piece by piece, she slipped further away from herself —
not because she was weak,
but because she thought she had to in order to be loved, accepted, or safe.

What she never knew is this:

Her true self is still there — waiting, untouched, unbroken.

Now it's your turn to guide her back home.

Write to the version of you who lost herself trying to survive.

Tell her it wasn't her fault.
Tell her she didn't choose wrong — she protected herself the only way she knew how.
Tell her you're ready to bring her back, gently and without pressure.

You may begin with:
"My love, you didn't lose yourself – you hid yourself to survive..."

Use these if you'd like a little guidance before writing your letter:

What parts of herself did she hide or silence?

Who or what made her feel like she had to disappear?

What parts of her do you miss the most?

How will you help her come back to herself now?

Letter to the Little Girl Who Lost Herself

Letter 6 — When She Looked for Approval

Before you begin writing, think of her gently —
the little girl who learned early that approval felt like love,
that praise felt like safety,
and that acceptance felt like belonging.

She wanted to be seen.
She wanted to be chosen.
She wanted someone to say,
"You're doing so well. I'm proud of you. You're enough just as you are."

But instead, she learned to measure her worth by what others thought.

This letter is for the girl who chased approval just to feel worthy.

A Gentle Introduction

She paid attention to everything —
faces, tones, reactions, moods.
She learned to perform, to perfect, to anticipate what people wanted from her.

Maybe she became the "good girl."
Maybe the achiever.
Maybe the helper.
Maybe the peacemaker.
Maybe the one who never caused trouble.

She thought approval was the doorway to love — and so she adapted herself again and again.

What she didn't know is this:

Approval is not proof of value.
She was valuable long before anyone noticed her.

Now it's your turn to tell her that.

Reflection Prompts

Write to the girl who tried to earn approval to feel safe and loved.

Tell her she didn't need to perform to be worthy.
Tell her her value was never up for negotiation.
Tell her you see her now — fully, clearly, lovingly.

You may begin with:
"My love, you never had to earn approval to deserve love..."

Use these if you'd like a little guidance before writing your letter:

Whose approval did she chase the most?

What did she think approval would give her?

How did seeking approval shape her identity?

What truth about worthiness do you want her to know now?

Letter to the Little Girl Who Looked for Approval

Letter 7 — When She Was Afraid

Before you write, hold her softly in your heart — the little girl who was often afraid, even when she tried not to show it.

Fear shows up differently in small bodies:
a tight chest, a quiet voice, tiptoeing around moods,
trying not to make mistakes,
trying to be "good,"
trying not to be noticed...
or trying so hard to be perfect.

This letter is for the girl who learned to live with fear she couldn't name.

A Gentle Introduction

She felt fear long before she had the words to explain it.
Fear of being hurt.
Fear of being ignored.
Fear of being in the way.
Fear of disappointing someone.
Fear of chaos, conflict, yelling, silence, or unpredictability.

Little girls aren't supposed to manage adult-sized worries —
but she did.

She navigated situations that felt too big for her small heart.
She tried to be brave, even when she was shaking inside.
She hid her fear because she thought she had to.

What she didn't know is this:

Fear doesn't make her weak —
it shows how much she survived.

Now you can offer her the safety she always needed.

Reflection Prompts

Write to the little girl who was afraid.

Tell her you understand why she felt the way she did.
Tell her her fear made sense.
Tell her she wasn't overreacting or too sensitive.
Tell her she deserved protection, reassurance, and calm.

You may begin with:
*"My love, you didn't imagine it – you were scared.
and you had every reason to be..."*

Use these if you'd like a little guidance before writing your letter:

What were her biggest fears?

How did she hide or cope with her fear?

Who should have comforted her, and what did she need to hear?

What would make her feel safe now?

Letter to the Little Girl Who Was Afraid

Letter 8 — When She Was Told to Shrink

Before you write, think softly of her — the little girl who was told, directly or quietly, that she needed to be **less.**

Less loud.
Less emotional.
Less opinionated.
Less curious.
Less demanding.
Less herself.

She learned to fold herself into smaller shapes
just to fit into the expectations around her.

This letter is for the girl who dimmed her light to make others comfortable.

A Gentle Introduction

There were moments she felt herself pulling inward — shrinking her voice, tucking away her brilliance, softening her truth because she didn't want to upset anyone.

Maybe she was told she was "too much."
Maybe she felt criticized for being expressive or imaginative.
Maybe she learned her needs weren't welcome.
Maybe she was praised only when she was quiet, agreeable, or small.

But the truth is:

She was never too much.
They were simply too limited to hold all of her.

She wasn't meant to shrink — she was meant to bloom.

Now you get to remind her of that.

Write to the little girl who was told to make herself smaller.

Tell her she deserved room to exist fully.
Tell her her emotions were valid.
Tell her her voice was meant to be heard.
Tell her she no longer has to apologize for taking up space.

You may begin with:
"My love, you were never 'too much.'
You were exactly who you were meant to be..."

Use these if you'd like a little guidance before writing your letter:

Who made her feel like she needed to shrink?

What parts of herself did she hide to be accepted?

What did she silence that deserved to be spoken?

How can you help her expand again now?

Letter to the Little Girl Who Was Told to Shrink

Letter 9 — When She Wanted to Believe in Herself

Before you begin writing, place her gently in your heart — the little girl who wanted to believe in herself... but wasn't always given the encouragement, confidence, or affirmation she needed.

She tried.
She hoped.
She imagined who she could become — but doubt often spoke louder than her dreams.

This letter is for the girl who needed someone to tell her she was capable, brilliant, and worthy of every good thing.

A Gentle Introduction

There were times she looked at the world with wonder, dreams tucked in her pockets, possibilities swirling through her small mind.

But she also looked at her reflection and asked:
"Can I really do this?"
"Am I smart enough?"
"Am I strong enough?"
"Will I fail?"

She didn't need to be perfect — she needed to be encouraged.

Maybe no one nurtured her gifts.
Maybe the people around her doubted themselves and passed that doubt onto her.
Maybe she grew up hearing criticism more than praise.
Maybe she learned to second-guess every part of herself.

What she never knew is this:

Her potential was never small —
she just needed someone to stand beside her and believe.

Now that someone is you.

Write to the little girl who struggled to believe in herself.

Tell her she is capable.
Tell her she is enough.
Tell her her dreams were never foolish — they were seeds.
Tell her she deserved voices that lifted her, not ones that made her shrink.

You may begin with:
"My love, you were always worthy of believing in yourself..."

Use these if you'd like a little guidance before writing your letter:

What dreams did she have that she was afraid to claim?

What made her doubt her abilities or worth?

What strengths did she have that no one acknowledged?

How can you help her believe in herself now, as the woman you've become?

Letter to the Little Girl Who Wanted to Believe in Herself

Letter 10 — When She Needed Comfort

Before you begin, take a slow breath.
Think of the little girl who needed comfort —
real comfort — not dismissal, not minimization,
not "you're fine,"
not "stop crying,"
not "be strong."

She needed arms.
She needed softness.
She needed someone to notice her pain, to acknowledge her feelings, to hold her without asking her to earn it.

This letter is for the girl who longed for comfort she didn't receive.

A Gentle Introduction

There were moments she was hurting inside, moments where her heart felt too heavy for her small body, moments she didn't have the words to express.

Maybe she cried quietly.
Maybe she hid her tears.
Maybe she learned to swallow her emotions because there was no space for them in the world around her.

She needed someone to sit beside her and say:
"I see you.
You're allowed to feel this.
It makes sense that you're hurting.
I'm here."

But she didn't get that. Not in the way she needed.
She didn't know that comfort is a birthright — not a luxury or a reward.

Now, you get to give her what she never had.

Reflection Prompts

Write to the little girl who needed comfort and didn't receive it.

Tell her her feelings were valid.
Tell her she didn't imagine the hurt.
Tell her she deserved warmth, softness, closeness, reassurance.
Tell her that it's okay to be human — she wasn't wrong
for needing comfort.

You may begin with:
"My love, you deserved someone to hold you when
you were hurting..."

Use these if you'd like a little guidance before writing your letter:

When did she need comfort the most?

How did she try to soothe herself when no one else did?

What emotions did she carry alone?

What comfort can you offer her now, as the woman you've become?

Letter to the Little Girl Who Needed Comfort

Letter 11 — When She Wanted to Start Over

Before you begin writing, imagine her —
the little girl who wanted a reset long before she even knew what that meant.
A do-over.
A fresh start.
A chance to rewrite the story around her.

Maybe she wished things were calmer.
Maybe she wished people were kinder.
Maybe she wished she could escape certain moments,
certain rooms,
certain versions of herself that were shaped by survival, not choice.

This letter is for the girl who longed for a new beginning.

A Gentle Introduction

Sometimes children carry silent wishes:
to move to a different home,
to wake up in a safer environment,
to have a different family dynamic,
to be understood,
to be loved properly,
to be allowed to exist without fear or pressure.

She didn't want a new life because she didn't love the one she had.
She wanted a new life because she deserved better.

And even though she couldn't start over then,
she can begin again now — through you.

You are her second chance.
You are her reset.
You are the beginning she prayed for in the quiet.

Write to the little girl who wished she could start over.

Tell her she wasn't wrong for wanting something different.
Tell her she wasn't ungrateful — she was intuitive.
Tell her you are creating a life now that honors her needs, dreams, and softness.

You may begin with:
"My love, I know you wished things could be different..."

Use these if you'd like a little guidance before writing your letter:

What did she want to start over from?

What parts of her life felt too heavy or too hard?

What new beginning did she dream of?

How are you giving her that new beginning now?

Letter to the Little Girl Who Wanted to Start Over

Letter 12— When She Needed You Most

Before you begin, place a hand over your heart.
Because this letter is the homecoming.
This one is for the little girl who needed you — not the world, not the people who failed her, not the ones who didn't understand her, but **you.**

She needed your voice.
Your comfort.
Your protection.
Your love.
Your presence.

She didn't know you yet — but she was waiting for you her entire childhood.

This is the letter she has been longing to hear.

A Gentle Introduction

There were moments she needed someone to sit beside her and say:

"I'm here."
"You didn't deserve that."
"You are safe now."
"You matter."
"You are allowed to feel this."
"I'm not going anywhere."

But no one said those words in the way she needed them, with the depth, the softness, the consistency that small hearts crave. She carried hurt alone. She carried confusion alone. She carried loneliness alone. She carried fears, dreams, secrets, and questions that were too heavy for her little body.

But she survived long enough to meet you — the one who can finally give her everything she needed.

Now, this letter becomes her safe place.

Write to the little girl who needed you most.

Tell her you're here now.
Tell her you will not abandon her.
Tell her you believe her.
Tell her she is loved, chosen, wanted, protected.
Tell her she doesn't have to face anything alone anymore.

*You may begin with: "My love, I'm here now...
and I won't leave you again."*

Use these if you'd like a little guidance before writing your letter:

When did she need someone the most?

What was she carrying that no one else saw?

What words would have saved her heart?

How will you show up for her from this point forward?

Letter to the Little Girl Who Needed You Most

PART III
THE BECOMING

THE BECOMING

You have written to the girl you once were.
You have held her, comforted her, listened to her, and given her back her voice.

Now, this section is about **you** —
the woman she grew into,
the woman she dreamed of,
the woman who survived, softened, and rose.

Becoming is not about becoming someone new.
It's about returning to who you were before the world told you otherwise.

Move through these prompts slowly.
Let them feel like a gentle awakening.

THE HEALING MIRROR

Healing is not only about remembering —
it's about seeing yourself clearly, gently, and truthfully
for the first time.

This section invites you to look into the mirror of your own heart
and reflect on what you've carried,
what you've healed,
and what you're ready to release.

Move slowly.
Let each question settle softly.
There are no wrong answers here.

Just honesty.
Just tenderness.
Just you.

What I Forgive Myself For

There are parts of your younger self that still need your forgiveness – not because she did anything wrong, but because she blamed herself for things that were never hers to carry.

What do you forgive her for?

What I No Longer Carry

There are stories that no longer belong to you. Beliefs that were never yours. Weights you were never meant to hold.

What are you finally ready to set down?

What I Now Understand

Time has given you perspective.
Softness has given you clarity.
Healing has given you truth.

What do you now understand about your childhood, your heart, and your journey?

What I Choose to Believe About Myself

This is your reclamation.
Your voice.
Your truth.

What do you choose to believe about yourself going forward?

What I Promise Myself Now

This is where healing becomes devotion.
This is where you gift your younger self — and your present self — a new beginning.

What promises are you ready to keep for yourself?

A LETTER TO THE WOMAN YOU ARE BECOMING

Beautiful woman,

You are not behind.
You are not late.
You are arriving — exactly on time.

Every version of you has been preparing the path for this moment.

For this opening.
For this becoming.

I hope you feel proud of the way you rise, even with trembling hands. I hope you see the light returning to your eyes.
Keep going, gently.

Your future self already thanks you.

Who I Am Now

You are no longer the girl who had to survive everything.
You are a woman who can choose softness, stillness, safety, love, truth.

Who are you now, in this season of your life?

What I Want Next

Your desires matter now.

Your dreams matter now.

Your voice matters now.

What do you want next — gentle, honestly, without shrinking?

What I Am Ready to Receive

You once had to survive without support, comfort, or softness.
But you are not that girl anymore.

What are you ready to receive now that you could not receive as a child?

Love? Rest? Help? Joy? Peace? Presence?

What I Am No Longer Available For

Healing brings boundaries.

Gentle, firm, sacred boundaries.

What are you no longer available for — emotionally, spiritually, relationally?

How I Will Care for My Inner Child Going Forward

She still lives inside you.
She still needs you.
She still trusts you.

How will you show up for her now, consistently, lovingly, fully?

The Woman I Am Becoming

This is where you step into your new beginning.
Not loudly.
Not forcefully.
But softly, intentionally, truthfully.

Who is the woman you are becoming?

My love,

If you are reading this, then you have done something extraordinary.

You have returned to the little girl inside you with open hands and an open heart.

You have listened to her whispers, her fears, her dreams.
You have held her with a gentleness she was once denied.
You have met her where she is — not where you wished she had been.

That is healing.
That is bravery.
That is love.

This journey was never about rewriting your childhood.
It was about reclaiming your story —
piece by piece, moment by moment, truth by truth.

And you did it.

You wrote the letters she needed.
You said the words she prayed for.
You gave her the protection, comfort, validation, and love she longed for in silence.

Now she is not alone.
Now she is not hidden.
Now she is not forgotten.

She has you.
Your voice.
Your softness.
Your strength.
Your truth.

And you — the woman reading these words — are no longer carrying the weight of a story you had to survive. You are stepping into the light of the story you are choosing to live.

So as you close these pages, I want to leave you with this:

You are allowed to grow.
You are allowed to rest.
You are allowed to receive love.
You are allowed to be soft.
You are allowed to be whole.
You are allowed to be held.
You are allowed to become everything she dreamed of and more.

Your past shaped you,
but it does not define you.

Your healing is yours.
Your future is yours.
Your softness is yours.

And the little girl inside you —
the one who survived,
the one who hoped,
the one who waited —
is finally home.

With all my love,
K. Nicol

NEXT STEPS FOR YOUR BECOMING

Your journey does not end with the last page.

It continues in the way you speak to yourself, choose yourself, and care for the girl you once were.

Here are gentle next steps:

- Revisit this workbook each season
- Write yourself a new letter every birthday
- Continue your Raised by 1912 healing legacy
- Share this space with another woman who needs it

Your becoming is lifelong.

And you deserve every soft step forward.

ABOUT THE AUTHOR

K. Nicol is a writer, attorney, and founder of Storyhouse™ — a creative and healing ecosystem anchored in tenderness, truth, lineage, and becoming. She holds a B.A. in Interdisciplinary Studies and an M.A. in Criminology, along with a Juris Doctorate, and spent decades serving as an investigator, prosecutor, and attorney.

Her work is shaped by the legacy of her grandmother, Mama (born in 1912), and by the inner worlds of women who learned to survive quietly while longing to be seen. Her background in social sciences, criminology, and trauma-informed work deepened her devotion to truth, humanity, and the emotional landscapes women carry.

Today, she uses storytelling as a form of healing — creating spaces for women to return to themselves with softness and permission.

Through Raised by 1912, Storyhouse™, and her reflective writing style, K. Nicol's work honors the girl you once were, the woman you are now, and the woman you are becoming.

She writes from Houston, Texas, where she is surrounded by her children, her creative work, and the legacy of women who came before her.

The Becoming — A Guided Journey Back to the Girl You Once Were
Written with warmth and intention by
K. Nicol

Created for the
Raised by 1912
healing legacy community
raisedby1912.com

This workbook was designed to honor:
the girl you once were,
the woman you are now,
and the lineage of softness, strength, and truth
that you are choosing to pass forward.

Thank you for allowing this space to hold your heart,
your memories,
your becoming.

May these pages continue to heal you
long after you close the book.

With love,
K. Nicol

Founder of Raised by 1912
& Storyhouse™

STORYHOUSE™ PUBLISHING IMPRINT STATEMENT

Storyhouse™ Publishing is the creative press of Storyhouse™, dedicated to producing beautifully crafted works that honor truth, memory, lineage, and becoming.
Every Storyhouse™ title is created with intention — shaped in softness, bound in legacy, and held with the belief that our stories are the quiet architecture of who we are.

All Storyhouse™ Publishing works are artfully developed, designed, and produced under the creative direction of **K. Nicol**, founder of Storyhouse™ and curator of Raised by 1912.

Published by
Storyhouse™ Publishing
A Storyhouse™ Imprint
storyhousepublishing.com

Printed in the United States of America.

STORYHOUSE™ PUBLISHING

Storyhouse™ Publishing
Where stories are shaped, held, and carried forward.

Founded by K. Nicol, Storyhouse™ Publishing is a boutique creative press dedicated to nurturing the voices, histories, and inner worlds of women who are rising into their truth.

Our mission is simple:
To create beautiful, intentional, emotionally resonant works that honor the past, celebrate the present, and illuminate the future.

We believe in:

- Softness as strength
- Storytelling as healing
- Legacy as love
- Words as home
- Women as authors of their own becoming

Under the Storyhouse™ umbrella, each book is crafted with tenderness, aesthetic intention, and a deep respect for the lived experiences that shape us.

Whether it is a guided journal, a memoir, or a quiet reflection piece, every Storyhouse™ publication is designed to feel like a companion — something you return to when you need grounding, clarity, or a gentle reminder of who you are.

Thank you for inviting Storyhouse™ Publishing into your healing journey.
It is our honor to hold space for your story.

Storyhouse™ Publishing
A division of Storyhouse™
storyhousepublishing.com

There is a girl you once were — the one who felt deeply, carried quietly, and waited her whole childhood for someone to return for her.

The Becoming is a guided, soulful journey back to that girl.

Through twelve beautifully crafted letters and a series of gentle, reflective prompts, this workbook invites you to reconnect with the younger version of yourself who survived more than she ever should have, who longed to be seen, who wanted to be loved, who waited for comfort, and who hoped you would come back for her someday.

Inside these pages, you will:

- Meet the girl you once were — with tenderness, honesty, and compassion
- Sit with her memories and emotions, without rushing or judgment
- Offer her the comfort, protection, and validation she deserved
- Reclaim the parts of yourself you hid to survive
- Release old stories that no longer belong to you
- Honor your inner child and her truth
- Step into the grounded, soft, powerful woman you are becoming

Written with exquisite emotional clarity and reverence for women's inner worlds, The Becoming is more than a workbook — it is a quiet homecoming. A return to the girl who remembers everything. A sanctuary for the truths you've carried. A soft, safe place to finally exhale.

This book does not ask you to be strong.
It asks you to be honest.
To be gentle.
To be present with yourself in ways you were not allowed to be as a child.

Move through these pages slowly.
Let each letter and reflection meet you where you are.
Your healing doesn't need urgency — only truth, tenderness, and permission.

This is your becoming.
And she has been waiting for you.

Made in the USA
Coppell, TX
23 December 2025